HELLO!

D0827429

Inspiring | Educating | Creating | Entertaining

Brimming with creative inspiration, how-to projects, and useful information to enrich your everyday life, Quarto Knows is a favorite destination for those pursuing their interests and passions. Visit our site and dig deeper with our books into your area of interest: Quarto Creates, Quarto Cooks, Quarto Homes, Quarto Lives, Quarto Drives, Quarto Explores, Quarto Gifts, or Quarto Kids.

Design: Emma Thyssen
Photography: Tatjana Matysik
Illustration: Emma Thyssen

Printed in China

MIX
Paper from
responsible sources
FSC® C104723

SARAH DEVOS

with illustrations by

emma thyssen

I AM

NEVER

BORED

The Best Ever Craft and Activity Book for Kids

✳ **100** Great Ideas for Kids to Do When There is Nothing to Do ✳

QUARRY

CONTENTS

THANKS

Anna and Rosie
for their always enthusiastic crafting help.

Sven
for putting up with a house full of
(and a wife who made) 100 crafts.

mama and my sisters
for the life-long craft inspiration and
the mental support.

oma and opa
for the support during busy times, the coffee
filter tip, and the speedy tubing and box delivery.

**the neighbor ladies, Emilia, Michiel and the
Vermeulen, Devel and Mallentjer families**
to the rescue.

all the kindergarten teachers that I know
eternal respect.

Emma, Frike, Elsie, Tatjana
and everyone who worked to make this into
another gem!

INTRODUCTION

Crafting: You've Got Lovers...and Haters

This is how it has always been and how it always will be. I've been a lover for as long as I can remember! I can still see the crafting books I used to leaf through as a kid so clearly in my head. And I had such fun putting this book together.

In doing so, the crafts my daughters made, tips from friends and family, Pinterest, and other crafting books provided a big source of inspiration—to which I often added my own twist. I hope you'll do that too! Change, cut, paste, and transform the crafts until they become your own. That's how you *really* start enjoying things (or at least I hope so).

I purposely avoided making the project examples too neat or too perfect. That's why I think this book might even change the minds of haters. **It doesn't need to be difficult, complicated, or expensive to make something beautiful or fun. And you don't have to graduate from art school to do this either.**

Because, what's probably not going to happen when you open this book?
- The crafts in the picture look so much more beautiful than anything you could ever make.
- You've slaved away for a half a day and haven't made anything that even remotely resembles what was promised in the book.
- You had to drive around for hours to buy all the supplies you need.
- After 10 minutes, you realize you're alone at the table while your kids are, um...not crafting.

So, what *is* the purpose of this book? To lay the groundwork for a fun afternoon! **Put out a snack, get your kids and yourself to the table, and get to work together. And don't worry about the mess or the spills. Your kids won't remember how clean you always kept the house, but they *will* remember the crafts you made together. They won't ever forget it.**

Have fun!

SARAH

P.S. Oh yeah, one other thing. No matter how enthusiastic—or perfectionistic—you are, let your child do the crafting him or herself. Making something is only fun when you do it yourself, duh! It makes you as proud as a peacock. Kids tend not to care whether or not their crafts end up looking blog-worthy, so long as they have fun in the process of making something and enjoy playing with something that they created themselves.

BEFORE YOU START

BE READY FOR...

MESS

Nope, you still can't make an omelet without breaking an egg. But there is hope! Here are a few tips for keeping things relatively tidy:

- Cut the bottom off of a plastic shopping bag. Pull it over your child's head, stick her arms through the handles, and you've got an apron. Or invest in a longer-lasting crafting apron—it'll pay for itself in no time.

- Squirt craft paint into an empty egg carton. That way you can just throw it out when you're done.

- Cover the table with a washable tablecloth and possibly put a large placemat on top.

- Make sure your workspace is close to soap and the sink (or make sure your child walks to the sink with his or her hands in a "stick 'em up!" pose).

HOARDING

Once you are on your way with this book, you'll never look at an empty toilet paper roll the same way. From now on, always keep:

Empty toilet paper rolls

Egg cartons

Craft sticks

Corks

Old socks

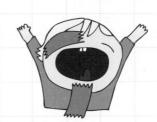

Oh, and cardboard boxes! Hooray for cardboard boxes!

ACUTE FRUSTRATION

Any time you're crafting, there might be a moment when one of the crafters becomes disgruntled. When it is *so* not going your way that it makes you cry. Or that you've been fiddling around with something for so long that you feel like catapulting your creation across the room. It happens. But whether or not it helps is another question. Might it perhaps be better to think of a solution? Or to ask someone for help? And who knows, a roadblock might even lead to a brand-new idea.

TONS OF FUN & LAUGHS

And that's what it's all about, right?

WHO CAN DO WHAT AND WHEN?

Frike van Nevel, child physiotherapist and Mama Boss expert, provides insight into what you can expect from your child and approximately when.

WHAT CAN YOU SEE, DO, AND ACCOMPLISH?

As a child, the interchange between what you can see, what you can do with your hands, and what you are trying to achieve is a work in progress. And of course, these are the three things you need to create beautiful crafts. Cutting, pasting, tearing, kneading, building, doing puzzles... These are all skills that require you to learn how to manage this interchange.

EVERYONE IS DIFFERENT

Learning all of these things doesn't just happen from one day to the next and no two children are completely alike. A great deal depends on interests and aptitudes—while one child might spend his or her time coloring neatly and carefully within the lines, another might race past you on his or her bike. So, there's no reason to panic if your child isn't great at something right off the bat. It's likely that he or she is just focused on something else at the moment and will learn that other skill later.

FOUR PHASES OF DEVELOPMENT

Here are a few guidelines to consider, but generally it's best to look at what your child is doing and how he or she handles things. Pick out an achievable craft together. This way, crafting will be an enjoyable activity for your child and one that is associated with a positive outcome—"Look what I made!" We tend to like doing things more when we are good at them and we tend to do things we like more often. Chicken or the egg!

AGE	SKILL	DEVELOPMENTAL PHASE
2 to 3½ years old	Guiding movements based on observation	Seeing and doing phase
3½ to 6 years old	Observation and knowing	Seeing and knowing phase
6 to 7 years old	Observation and reasoning	Seeing and thinking phase
8 years old and up	Reasoning	Thinking phase

SEEING AND DOING PHASE

2 to 3½ years old—
perceptual-motor phase

Toddlers begin to understand concepts like soft, warm, cold, thick, and thin. The child adapts his or her behavior to what is heard or seen or done with the hands.

Good things to try now: puzzles, finger painting, tearing paper, crumpling paper, cutting with safety scissors

SEEING AND THINKING PHASE

6 to 7 years old—
perceptual-conceptual phase

Starting elementary school! A big step, as learning to write requires dexterity. Concrete materials are still needed to help develop spatial reasoning. Crafting can be a fun way to work on this. Without concrete materials, concepts like more, less, between, and behind become very difficult to understand. Children at this age are capable planners and are able to consider their approach to a task

Good things to try now: building according to instructions, drawing, tracing, Perler or stitch beads, sculpting with clay, cutting, pasting, piercing, folding, copying something in sections and putting it together to make a whole

SEEING AND KNOWING PHASE

3½ to 6 years old—
perceptual phase

Pre-schoolers and kindergarteners become acquainted with shapes and figures. They enjoy working with concrete materials to make beautiful things. Real board games also come into play in this phase.

Good things to try now: puzzles, dominoes, bingo, salt dough, clay, plasticine, coloring, pasting

THINKING PHASE

From 8 years old onward—
conceptual phase

Around the third grade, kids become less dependent upon concrete material until they no longer need it. They are capable of envisioning changes in color, form, direction, size, and thickness in their thoughts. An example can now be built in another format or size. What's great is that our development in this phase continues throughout our entire lives!

Good things to try now: thought puzzles, more complex projects, building

NO STRESS!

Once again: The ages specified here are guidelines only. Have a look at how your child carries out a task and which steps he or she takes to bring the task to completion. This is more important than adhering to the ages and phases listed here.

Have you noticed that your child is really having trouble with crafting? Make an appointment with a psychomotor therapist or an occupational therapist. They are qualified to assess your child's abilities and will intervene if necessary with therapy or simply provide advice as to what you can do to develop particular skills at home in a playful manner.

WHAT'S IN YOUR CRAFT CUPBOARD?

The following are handy items to always have nearby for a chronic case of craft-itis.

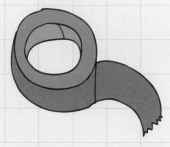

CRAFTING SUPPLIES:

- Drawing paper in various colors
- Crêpe paper
- Tissue paper
- Craft paint
- Fabric scraps
- Wool scraps
- Embroidery thread
- Fishing line
- A thick, black, permanent marker

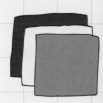

THINGS THAT STICK:

- Craft glue
- All-purpose glue
- Glue stick
- Tape
- Washi tape
- Duct tape

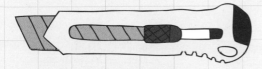

FOR THE MORE
SKILLED CRAFTERS:

- Darning needle
- Scissors
- Linchpins
- Utility knife
- Hole punch
- Stapler

ALSO NICE TO HAVE:

- Stick-on googly eyes
- Pipe cleaners
- Perler beads
- Clay
- Rope and string
- Fake feathers
- Glitter
- Beads in different sizes, materials, and colors

*

TIP!
I can't go without my thick, black markers. The addition of a couple of black lines can make your crafts so much cooler and can add so much more expression to a face (by outlining the eyes, for example). Give it a try!

KNOW YOUR
CLASSICS

Do you have crafting memories? I do. Instant flashbacks to salt dough and a garlic press. And at school, there wasn't a holiday that went by without all of us working industriously on paper chains. What's fun is that you can experience it all over again now—with a child's sparkling eyes right next to you.

1 MAGIC DRAWING PAPER

That wonderful moment when you reveal the colors from underneath a thick layer of black paint...unforgettable. Magic drawing paper for the win!

SUPPLIES

- **drawing paper**
- **crayons**
- **black poster paint (or another dark color)**
- **thick paintbrush**
- **something to scratch with (e.g. toothpick)**

① Color the sheet of paper *completely* using crayons. The colors can overlap, as long as there isn't a speck of white left on the sheet of paper.

② Paint the sheet of paper completely black. It might need a second coat.

③ Allow the paint to dry fully. Speed this up by putting the paper near a heater or in the sun.

④ Using a toothpick, scratch out a drawing in the black paint.

 Also makes a unique greeting card!
TIP!

2 SALT DOUGH

Good news: The ingredients for salt dough are things you will usually have on hand. And putting some in your mouth isn't an issue (but one bite will likely be enough).

SUPPLIES

- **2 to 3 cups (250 to 375 g) of flour**
- **1 cup (235 ml) water**
- **1 cup (300 g) salt**
- **1 tablespoon (15 ml) plant-based oil (e.g. sunflower oil)**
- **cookie cutters, optional**

① Mix all the dough ingredients together fully.

② Too crumbly? Add more water. Too wet? A bit more flour.

③ Flatten the dough and cut shapes, roll it into sausages, or think of your own sculptures.

④ Bake the finished products on a baking sheet in a 210°F (100°C) oven. The thicker the item being baked, the longer the cooking time. It can take anywhere from an hour to several hours. You can also leave them to dry by the heater, but this will take even longer.

⑤ Want to give your masterpieces a little sheen? Brush them with a bit of oil before baking. If you want to give them a bit of color, paint them *after* baking. We made a stars-and-moon mobile and painted the hangers with glow-in-the-dark paint. How cool is that?

★ TIP! Use a garlic press to make fun hair for your sculptures.

3 PAPER HAT

Always forget how to fold one of these? No worries. Here's the cheat sheet.

SUPPLIES

• **sheet of paper or old newspaper**

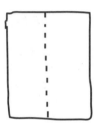

①
Fold the paper in half lengthwise to crease it and then unfold.

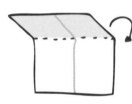

②
Fold the paper in half widthwise and don't unfold it. Place the folded paper in front of you with the open end facing you.

③
Fold the top corners toward the middle, against the crease made with the first fold in step 1.

④
Fold the bottom edge of the paper upward, over the triangles.

⑤
Flip the paper over and fold the bottom edge of the other side upward, over the triangles.

4 OLD-SCHOOL LANTERNS

A lot of ambiance for very little money.

SUPPLIES

- **tissue paper**
- **scissors**
- **paintbrush**
- **crafting glue**
- **1 empty glass jar (without lid)**
- **1 tea light**

① Cut the tissue paper into small square or rectangular pieces. If the lantern is for a specific holiday or themed party, be sure to use the appropriate colors.

② Using the paintbrush, coat part of the glass jar with glue and stick some of the tissue paper squares onto the jar. Press them down well. It doesn't matter if glue gets on top of the paper during this process. You won't be able to see it when it dries. Make sure that the tissue paper squares overlap if you want to cover the entire glass jar. Stick the tissue paper squares on in neat rows, a special shape, or no particular pattern at all.

③ Continue until the entire glass jar is covered with tissue paper and allow it to dry completely. Place a tea light inside and enjoy the ambiance.

5 BIRD FEEDER

At the end of fall, you can give the neighborhood birds a taste of the food you plan to offer them next season. Then you can make peanut garlands for them all winter long!

- **darning needle**
- **yarn**
- **unshelled peanuts**
- **thick piece of felt or corkboard, optional**

①

Thread the needle with the yarn. Tie the loose end with a double knot.

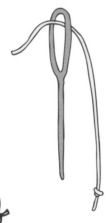

②

Place a peanut on a piece of felt or corkboard and pierce it with the needle. Big kids can just carefully hold the peanut.

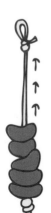

③

Continue until the length of yarn is filled with peanuts. Tie off the garland on the top end with a double knot as well and hang it in a tree or on a balcony. Be sure to place it high enough so that cats can't reach the happily feeding birds!

6 PAPER CHAINS

A golden oldie.

SUPPLIES

- colored paper
- scissors
- glue
- tape or a stapler, optional

①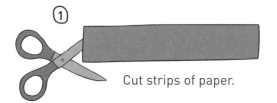

Cut strips of paper.

② Close the first ring with glue, tape, or a staple.

③ All the rest of the strips should be linked through the previous ring before being glued, taped, or stapled closed.

⭐ Great as a party garland, decoration, or for
TIP! the Twisted-Paper Caterpillar on page 99!

7 MMMARZIPAN

Before you can say the word "marzipan," it'll already be finished! (And maybe also eaten, but *that* we have nothing to do with.)

SUPPLIES

- **4 cups (250 g) confectioner's sugar**
- **4 cups (250 g) almond flour (or make your own by grinding whole or slivered almonds)**
- **¼ cup (60 ml) water**
- **1 teaspoon lemon juice**
- **vanilla extract, optional**
- **cacao powder or food coloring, optional**

① Sift the confectioner's sugar into the almond flour and mix.

② Add the water, the lemon juice, and the vanilla extract (to taste).

③ Mix well until a smooth, thick paste is formed.

④ Want to make brown marzipan? Add a bit of cacao powder to the mixture (or food coloring for another color). Roll the marzipan into balls or make it into snowmen, pigs, or other figures.

★ Dip the noses in melted chocolate.

TIP! Use chocolate chips for eyes.

WOOLLY WINTER

Pajamas, nicely preheated on the radiator. The smell of gingerbread and hot chocolate. New winter slippers and looking forward to all the festive holiday lights. Opening gifts and singing carols. We heart woolly winters.

8 CANDY CRACKERS

In England, people typically give each other this explosive little gift during the holidays, but you can certainly make them any time of year.

SUPPLIES

- 1 empty toilet paper roll
- tissue paper, approx. 5" × 10" (13 x 26 cm)
- wrapping paper, approx. 4" × 5" (10 x 13 cm)
- glue
- ribbon
- candy or small trinkets
- scissors, optional
- tape, optional

① Apply lengthwise lines of glue to the toilet paper roll.

② Lay the tissue paper, widthwise, on the table. Place the toilet paper roll on the bottom edge, centered, and roll away toward the top of the sheet—the paper will stick to the glue on the toilet paper roll. There should be excess paper on both the left and right ends.

 Apply glue to the edges of the reverse side of the wrapping paper. Place the wrapping paper lengthwise on the table and roll the toilet paper roll (centered on the wrapping paper sheet) until the wrapping paper is stuck all the way around.

④ Tie a piece of ribbon around the excess tissue paper on one end, making a bow.

⑤ Fill the cracker with candies or small trinkets.

⑥ Tie the other end closed with ribbon and let the festivities begin!

9 GLOWING SNOWMEN

Oh! How cute can snowmen actually be?

SUPPLIES

- **LED tea lights**
- **black permanent marker**
- **decorations: small pompoms, red ribbon, pipe cleaners, paper, etc.**
- **all-purpose glue**

① Draw two black dots above the LED flame (aka, the snowman's nose) to make the eyes. Then draw several dots under the nose to make the mouth.

② Decorate the snowman any way you'd like:

- earmuffs: glue a red ribbon over the top part of the head and apply mini-pompoms on either side, left and right;
- top hat and tie: cut a hat and tie out of paper and glue them to the top and bottom of the head, respectively;
- reindeer: glue a black or brown pipe cleaner to the back of the tea light and bring it forward, twisting it a bit at the top;
- winter hat: cut a hat out of paper, glue it to the top, and finish it off with a mini-pompom and a bit of pipe cleaner.

10 STAINED GLASS WINDOW WITH TISSUE PAPER

Fairy tale shadows for your window.

SUPPLIES

- black drawing paper
- large strips of tissue paper in various colors
- pencil
- scissors
- glue
- utility knife
- string or fishing line

① Decide on the shape of the window. Draw the shape in pencil on the paper. Lay a second sheet of black drawing paper under the first and cut out two of the same shape at once.

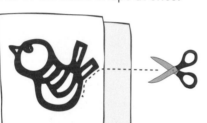

② Use a utility knife to make openings in one or both shapes. It's enough just to cut out the outline of the shape (and not the openings). Looking to be super precise? Cut exactly the same openings into the second figure that you did into the first.

③ First glue the strips of tissue paper to the back of one shape. You can even use two or more colors for one opening.

④ Then trim the excess tissue paper off the sides.

⑤ Glue the second shape to the back of the "stained glass window" for support.

TIP! Stained glass windows often have a frame. You can make one too. Cut out the shape and the frame separately and glue them back together at the end. This makes the process of cutting out and making openings a bit easier.

11 CUT-OUT SNOWFLAKES

Not quite as good as fresh, powdery snow, but not a bad second choice.

SUPPLIES

- **white paper (preferably square)**
- **scissors**
- **washi tape, optional**

①
Fold the paper in half once and then in half again.

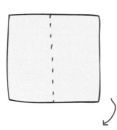

②
Cut shapes into the sides of the paper. Try and experiment with stripes, half hearts, circles. You can also cut into the middle of the paper. Just make sure that the paper remains attached in at least one place.

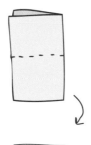

③
Unfold the paper. Happy with your snowflake? Hang it up in the window with a festive piece of washi tape.

12 SUPER SNOW GLOBE

Whether it's a classic figurine, an ornament made out of Perler beads, or a laminated picture inside, a snow globe is and will always be the best!

SUPPLIES

- **1 clean, empty glass jar with lid**
- **wintery figurine or other item**
- **strong all-purpose glue**
- **water**
- **glitter or glitter snow**
- **glycerine**
- **strong tape, optional**

① Remove the lid from the jar. Set up the figurines on the inside of the lid and glue them down well. Allow to dry.

② Meanwhile, fill the jar with water, some glitter, and a couple of drops of glycerine. Start by adding a little and add more until you're satisfied with the result.

③ Tightly screw the lid back on the jar and you're finished!

④ Want to decrease the risk of the jar opening by accident? Seal the lid closed with strong tape.

13 CRAZY CORK MEN

When the champagne corks are flying, make sure to dive under the table right away to collect them all. Because who doesn't want to ring in the new year with these cork men in their home?

- **a bunch of corks**
- **small balloons**
- **permanent markers**

①
Cut off a piece of the opening of the balloon, just enough so that you can pull the opening over the top of the cork.

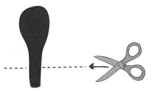

② Pull the balloon over the uppermost part of the cork. The very top will be your man's balloon nose.

③
Draw a crazy, happy, sad, or mad face on the balloon.

14 MONSTROUS PIGGY BANK

Your money will be safe in here!

SUPPLIES

- **1 empty cylindrical container (from Pringles chips, for example)**
- **paper and cardboard**
- **glue**
- **felt marker**
- **scissors or a utility knife**

①

Coat the container with glue and wrap it in nice paper. Make sure that the paper covers the entire container and that it sticks well.

②

Just above halfway up the container, draw a monstrous mouth. Cut the inside of the mouth out so that there is an opening into the container.

③

Draw the monster's eyes, the contours of its mouth, and any other details you'd like. Or draw on a piece of paper first and stick it onto the container after.

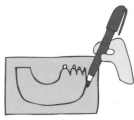

④ Draw two (or more) arms on a leftover piece of cardboard or thick paper and cut them out. Cut appropriately sized slots in the sides of the monster and insert the arms.

MARKER

15 PENGUIN COLONY

Penguins like to live in big groups. Better get to work!

SUPPLIES

- **1 empty egg carton**
- **white and black paint**
- **paintbrush**
- **thick orange or yellow paper**
- **scissors**
- **glue**
- **googly eyes**

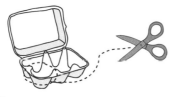

(1) Cut one of the individual egg holders out of the egg carton. Don't worry too much about the edges. You can trim them later.

(2) Paint a white half circle on the front. This will be the penguin's belly. Paint the rest of the carton black. Allow to dry completely.

(3) If there's any extra carton on the bottom, now is the time to trim it off neatly.

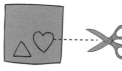

(4) Cut a small triangle out of the colored paper. This will be the beak. Glue the triangle onto the penguin, just above his white belly. Glue the googly eyes above the beak.

(5) Now cut a heart out of the colored paper. Fold the point of the heart over and glue the flap to the inside of the carton. This will serve as the penguin's feet.

⭐ **TIP!** The upward-facing points in the center of the egg carton make good icebergs. Paint them white or an icy light blue.

16 GOOD-LUCK DOLLS

Of course, you can buy these readymade, but homemade ones are so much more fun.

SUPPLIES
- **fine string (with a tassel on the end)**
- **wooden beads (different colors, shapes, and sizes)**
- **permanent marker**
- **extra decorations, optional**

①

If there isn't already a knot at the end of the string, make one now.

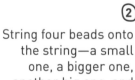

②

String four beads onto the string—a small one, a bigger one, another big one, and then a smaller one, for example. Then tie another knot to keep the beads in place.

③

Draw a face on the bead that is meant to be the head (or just two dots as a pair of eyes).

④

Decorate the doll with drawings, heart stickers, or other fun things.

17 WINTER BEARD

A great way to stay warm!

SUPPLIES

- **a piece of light fabric**
- **elastic**
- **1 bag of cotton balls**
- **scissors**
- **stapler**
- **glue**

① Cut the shape of a beard out of the fabric. Make an opening for the mouth as well.

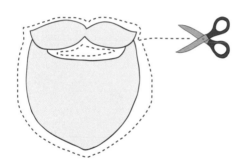

② Measure out a length of elastic that fits around the beard wearer's head. Staple the ends to the fabric beard at the height of the mustache.

③ Glue cotton balls onto the beard. Make sure to place them close together so that they fully cover the fabric.

④ Allow the glue to dry and try on the beard!

KNOW YOUR
CLASSICS

Many crafting techniques—
rolling "ropes" out of clay, spattering
paint, potato stamps—have remained
surprisingly popular over the years. Even
a simple fortune teller or a TV (made
of cardboard, of course) will keep your
children entertained for hours!

18 EMBROIDERED STARS

Make a star, not war!

SUPPLIES

- **embroidery thread**
- **thick needle**
- **thick paper**
- **pencil**
- **hole punch, optional**

① Thread the embroidery thread through the needle and tie a knot on one end.

② Think of a shape to embroider, *Ursa Minor* (the Little Dipper), for example, or a star shape. Draw the shape on the sheet of paper using a pencil.

③ Mark the points at which the needle will perforate the paper. For the nicest result, place two points next to each other. This way the thread won't end up being more prominent on the back of the paper and the shape will be clearer.

④ Use the hole punch to make the holes, or simply begin embroidering with the needle. Start in such a way that the knot in the thread stays on the back of the sheet of paper.

⑤ Be sure to end on the back of the sheet of paper as well. Tie a knot in the thread and trim it off.

19 FORTUNE TELLER

Our all-time favorite when it comes to nostalgia for our youth.

SUPPLIES
• paper
• markers, crayons, or colored pencils

① Fold the fortune teller according to the instructions below. Next, draw shapes or colored dots on every section on the inside. Underneath the flaps, write answers to the question "who or what am I?" Think up all sorts of crazy answers, like "a pancake," "amazing," or "the gymnastics teacher."

A 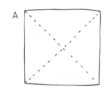 B C 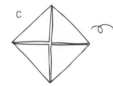 D

E 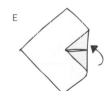 F G H

② Place your thumbs and index fingers in the spaces underneath.

③ Ask someone to say a number. Open the fortune teller that many times, alternating between sideways and up and down. Ask the person to choose a shape (or color or figure). Open that flap and read the answer to what (or who) he or she is.

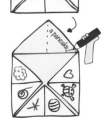

20 CARDBOARD TV

Watching the news has never been this much fun!

SUPPLIES

- **1 large cardboard box**
- **scissors or utility knife**
- **thick markers**

①

Place the box on the table, with the open side facing down. If the box still has flaps on the open side, cut these off. It makes it easier to work with.

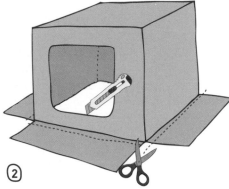

③

Draw a few buttons and decorations on the TV.

②

Cut a (rounded) square opening into the front of the box.

④

Stick your head into the underside of the box and let the show begin!

 TIP! It's even more fun to make signs saying, "Evening News," "Commercials," or whatever else you can think of. Of course, you can also make a remote control out of cardboard!

21 CLAY POTS
Nostalgia!

SUPPLIES • **modeling clay**

There are two easy ways to make a clay pot.

PUSH OUT A POT
Make a ball out of a handful of clay (about the size of a snowball). Press into the ball with both thumbs to make a hollowed-out area in the center of the ball. Keep making it bigger. Make the sides of the pot thinner and thinner until you are happy with the way the pot looks. Wet your fingers with water if the clay starts to dry out. If necessary, flatten out the bottom of the pot so that it stands up properly.

ROLL A POT
Make a flat, round disc out of clay for the bottom of the pot. Then, roll several "noodles" and stack them on top of each other around the outside edge of the base. Make sure that the ends of the "noodles" overlap. (If they don't, and the ends are all in the same place, the pot will be weak in that spot.) Keep going until the pot is tall enough. Wet your fingers with water and press the "noodles" more firmly against each other.

TIP! Is the pot stuck to the work surface? Removing it is easy with a bit of metal wire, pulled tight and slipped underneath the base. No wire in the house? Dental floss will work, too.

22 PERLER BEADS

Coasters that do double duty as anti-bug covers?
Fantastic invention.

SUPPLIES
- **Perler beads and peg board**
- **special ironing paper or parchment paper**
- **iron**

① Place the beads in a circle (about 3 inches [7 to 8 cm] in diameter) on the peg board. Leave a small hole in the middle that will fit a drinking straw.

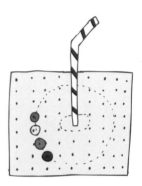

② When you are satisfied with the design, iron the beads (with the ironing paper on top) until they melt and bind together. It takes a bit of trial and error to figure out just how long to iron the beads, but it is usually about 20 seconds. Make sure to check the beads' progress as you iron to make sure they haven't melted more quickly.

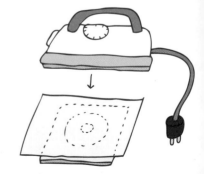

③ Allow the beads to cool and use them as a coaster or on top of a glass as a lid with a straw through it.

23 POTATO STAMPS

Another all-time favorite. Roll up your sleeves and...stamp!

SUPPLIES
- **large potatoes**
- **paring knife**
- **paint**
- **plate or paper plate**
- **paper**

① Slice a potato in half, lengthwise.

② Using the point of the paring knife, carve a simple shape into the flesh of the potato. Think star, heart, circle, or triangle.

③ Now remove the layer of the potato that surrounds the shape.

④ Pour a small amount of paint onto a plate, press the potato stamp into the paint, and then stamp away on a piece of paper. You can always do a test stamp first.

⑤ Want to use another color? Rinse the potato stamp off under the tap, pat it dry, and you're back in action.

 TIP! Don't have a steady hand? Use a cookie cutter to cut a shape into your potato.

An apple or onion cut in half also make good stamps. Just dip them in paint as is, stamp, and draw on a stem and leaf.

24 PAINT SPLATTER ART

Spraypaint—the easy way.

SUPPLIES
- **thick paper**
- **2 old toothbrushes**
- **liquid watercolor paint**
- **scissors**

① Cut out a stencil from the paper—a flower, word, or star, for example. Lay the stencil on top of another sheet of paper or a greeting card.

②

Dip one toothbrush into the paint, rub the bristles with the other toothbrush, and let the paint splatter onto and around the stencil. You can splatter different colors of paint on top of each other or around each other, as well as use different stencils, one after the other. Just make sure that the stencil doesn't slip out of place!

★ **TIP!** For best results, avoid using too much paint. Paint splatters are likely to get on your clothes and hands.

③ Let the artwork dry and then carefully remove the stencil.

SUPER SPRING

And just when the woolly winter is starting to feel a bit tired (all right, all right...you've been looking forward to spring for weeks), little green leaves start peeking out, baby chicks arrive, and playing dress-up and spring parties no longer seem so far away. Hooray! Spring is in the air!

25 PAPER BAG MASKS

Making masks can be complicated. Luckily, making these paper bag masks is not.

SUPPLIES

- **1 brown paper bag (preferably plain, without text)**
- **scissors**
- **felt pens**
- **drawing paper in various colors**
- **decorations, optional**

① Pull the paper bag on over your head and feel where your eyes are. Take the bag off and cut two eye holes in the designated locations.

② Make a scary, funny, or crazy face for the bag monster. Additional decoration is allowed!

③ Put the paper bag on again and announce the official opening of Paper Bag Monster City.

 TIP! Don't have any paper bags at home? A cardboard box will work too!

26 FEATHER CROWN

Whether you're heading to a spring fling or a carnival, a feather crown makes any outfit Instagram worthy.

SUPPLIES

- **2 long strips of strong fabric (I used denim)**
- **measuring tape**
- **fabric scissors**
- **glue**
- **a few novelty feathers or real feathers**
- **self-adhering Velcro**

①
Measure your head circumference. Err on the bigger side—better off too long than too short! You can adjust the fit later using the Velcro.

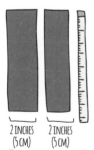

② Cut two strips of fabric in the desired length. The crown in the photo is about 2 inches (5 cm) wide.

2 INCHES (5 CM)   2 INCHES (5 CM)

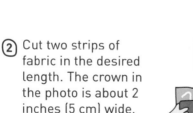

⑤ Flip the other strip of fabric over and press both strips together. Allow to dry fully.

④ Place the feathers in any pattern on the glue.

⑥ Cut a length of Velcro. Stick one side of the Velcro onto the end of the fabric strip on the outside and then stick the other side of the Velcro onto the inside of the other end of the crown. This way, the crown can be adjusted to fit any and every little head.

③ Lay the strips of fabric, good-side down, on the table. Coat one with glue.

27 MUSTACHE

I don't know what it is about this mustache, but it always makes us laugh.

- **yarn or wool**
- **scissors**
- **elastic cord**

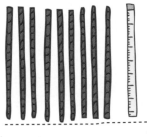

(1) Cut a whole bunch of pieces of yarn or wool, each about 4 inches (10 cm) in length, until you feel like it's thick enough for a mustache.

(3)

Thread the elastic cord underneath this knot and tie it around your head.

(2) Place the lengths of yarn next to each other and tie them together in the middle using another piece of yarn.

⭐ **TIP!** Even more hilarious paired with a fake nose (a piece of paper rolled up into a cone shape).

28 BLOWN EGGS

You can also just dye your eggs whole, of course, but when they're blown, you can keep them forever.

SUPPLIES

- **eggs**
- **skewer**
- **darning needle or sharp knife**
- **bowl**

① Use the needle to poke small holes into the top and bottom of the egg.

② The hole on the bottom of the egg (the widest end) can be made bigger, if necessary, by inserting a skewer into it. You can also use the skewer to puncture the yolk on the inside to make blowing out the contents of the egg easier.

③ Blow into the hole on the top of the egg, making sure the yolk and white end up in a bowl (omelet, anyone?).

④ Rinse the blown egg thoroughly, and blow out any excess water.

⑤ Let the eggs dry overnight. Then they'll be ready to decorate (see next page).

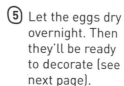

29 DECORATED EGGS

Go nuts!

SUPPLIES

- eggs (whole or blown)
- fine-point markers, natural dyes (see below), tattoos...

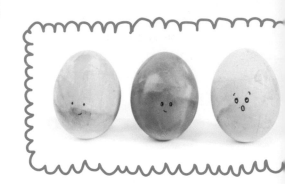

①

Want to eat your eggs after coloring them? Before you boil the eggs, add the following ingredients to the cooking water. Let them soak a bit longer in the water for a brighter color.

RED BEET	RED CABBAGE	TURMERIC
PINK	**BLUE**	YELLOW

②

If you're using blown eggs (see previous page), you can get started with decorating right away. You can paint your egg, draw on it, or even carefully apply a tattoo or stickers on it! The tattoo trick also works on cooled, hardboiled eggs.

TIP! Quail's eggs look even cuter when they're pastel colored. And they're extra tasty when eaten with a dip made of mayonnaise, yogurt, pepper, and salt.

30 MINI BASKETS

A basket for every guest at the brunch table, with a bit of bread or tasty cookies in it. One to keep your eggs in. Or just as decoration. You decide.

SUPPLIES

- 1 paper plate
- scissors
- tape
- paper in a nice print or ribbon
- washi tape
- white and pink paper

- 3 short white pipe cleaners
- white or pink mini-pompoms
- glue
- black marker

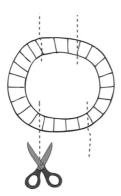

① Make two cuts into the top and bottom of the paper plate.

② Fold the sides inward to make a basket shape and secure with tape.

③

Glue a piece of paper around the bottom of the basket. Decorate with washi tape.

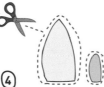

④ Cut ears out of the white paper and glue a smaller, pink oval onto the inside. Glue the ears on the inside of the front of the basket with the pink side facing out.

⑤ Draw the bunny's eyes.

⑥ Twist the pipe cleaners around each other in the middle and glue them under the eyes. Glue a pompom on top for the nose.

31 DOILY SHEEP

Baa! Care to join me in the meadow?

SUPPLIES

- **colored drawing paper, including black**
- **googly eyes**
- **small doilies**
- **scissors**
- **glue**

① Cut a sheep's head out of the black paper.

② Glue two googly eyes onto the head and glue the head onto a doily.

③ Cut out two black rectangles for the legs (yes, sheep have four legs, but the other two are hidden here) and glue them onto the back of the doily.

④ Glue the sheep on a sheet of paper to start filling the meadow with an entire flock.

32 HAPPY BEES

For a beeeautiful, happy table!

SUPPLIES

- **1 toilet paper roll**
- **scissors**
- **yellow paint and paintbrush**
- **1 cotton ball**
- **black marker**
- **1 wooden skewer**
- **1 black pipe cleaner**
- **glue**

① Cut off a "ring" from the toilet paper roll that is about ¾ inch (2 cm) wide. Paint the inside and the outside of the ring yellow.

② Fold six equal points into the ring so that it takes on the shape of a honeycomb.

③ Paint the cotton ball yellow. Allow to dry fully.

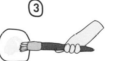

④ Draw black strips and a face on the cotton ball.

⑤ Using the wooden skewer, poke a hole through the cotton ball.

⑥ Cut off two short pieces of pipe cleaner, bend them into loops, and insert them into the openings on either side to make wings.

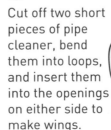

⑦ Glue the bee onto the "honeycomb" and carefully insert a napkin into the ring.

⭐ **TIP!** Feel like making a whole hive? Glue a bunch of honeycomb rings together.

33 ALMOST-REAL MOUNTED BUTTERFLIES

Because it's more fun to let the live ones keep flapping their wings.

SUPPLIES

- **thick drawing paper or watercolor paper**
- **fine-point felt pen**
- **watercolor paint**
- **paintbrush**
- **deep frame**
- **scissors**
- **small straight pins or glue**

① Cut a butterfly form out of the paper. Make sure that it fits in the frame that it needs to go in later.

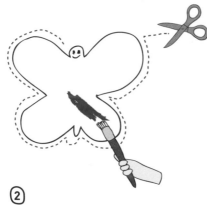

② Draw a face on the butterfly using a pen and then paint the butterfly with watercolors. Use your imagination. Give your butterfly polka dots, stripes, or wild colors. You'll think of something! Allow the paint to dry fully.

③ Carefully pin or glue the butterfly into the frame. The wings should not sit completely flat against the back of the frame. This makes the butterfly look more realistic.

④ Is the frame large? Make several butterflies and pin them neatly next to, above, or below each other.

KNOW YOUR

CLASSICS

In the spring, it's not unusual to suddenly have the urge to change everything in your house or your room. You move the couch somewhere else and then it's time for wholesale spring cleaning. Everything needs to feel new and fresh and tidy! Macramé plant hangers (totally hip), crocheted garlands, and homemade placemats are exactly what you need here. Don't feel like that at all? Then just gallop away on your hobby horse!

34 QUICK HOBBY HORSE

Yee haw, cowboys and cowgirls!

- **thick paper or thin cardboard**
- **1 broomstick, branch, or bamboo stake from the garden**
- **paint or markers**
- **scissors**
- **tape, glue, or stapler**
- **wool remnants**

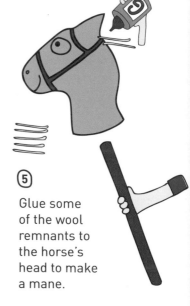

① Lay two sheets of paper on top of each other, draw the shape of a horse's head, and cut the shape out of both sheets of paper.

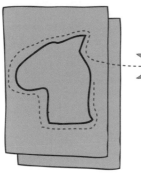

④ Insert the stick into the opening.

② Draw an eye, mouth, and any other details on both sides.

③

Glue the two sides of the horse's head together along the edges, leaving an opening at the bottom.

⑤

Glue some of the wool remnants to the horse's head to make a mane.

35 MACRAMÉ OLÉ!

Plant hangers with knotted strings are back in style! Thankfully, it doesn't have to be expensive or difficult to be trendy.

SUPPLIES

- **4 pieces of string, each about 6½ feet (2 meters) long, doubled up**
- **1 wooden or metal ring or key ring**
- **scissors**
- **flowerpot, approx. 4 to 6 inches (10 to 15 cm) in diameter, with a plant**

① Lay the four doubled up pieces of string on top of each other and tie them in the middle to the ring with a double knot. Don't have a ring? Tie the strings to the door handle.

② Take two strings and tie them in a knot about 14 inches (35 cm) from the double knot at the top. Do the same with the other six strings, making four knots in total. Try to tie all of the knots at the same height to ensure the best-looking result.

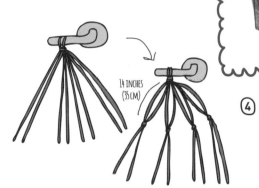

14 INCHES (35 CM)

③ Next, make a new series of knots about 4 inches (10 cm) lower than the previous ones. Take note: The idea here is to tie the rightmost string from the first knot to the leftmost string from the next first knot. What you're doing is tying each string to its neighbor. Keep going until you've tied another four knots, all of which should again be at the same height.

4 INCHES (10 CM)

TIE TO EACH OTHER

④ Repeat the previous step, this time another 4 inches (10 cm) lower. Just underneath the last knot, tie all the strings together again in a big double knot. Place the flowerpot in the hanger and hang up this homemade creation.

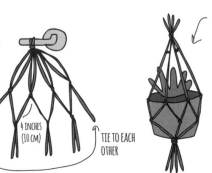

⭐ **TIP!** Already mastered this technique? The Internet is full of instruction manuals for making more complicated knots.

36 LINE DRAWING

Remember this one?

SUPPLIES
- **pen**
- **paper**

1 Randomly draw a few circles on a sheet of paper.

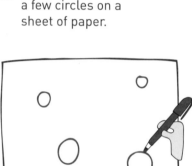

2 Then, fill the sheet of paper with horizontal lines, drawing around each circle so that you create waves in the line drawing.

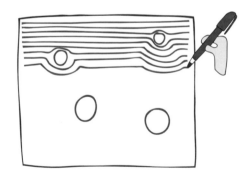

3 It's always fun to make the line drawing into something more. Maybe the circles are monster eyes in a cave? Or birds on a wire?

37 ZIGZAG BOOK

A homemade book is a great place to record your vacation memories or to keep your funniest photos or quotes in. It also makes a lovely gift.

- thick paper or cardboard
- utility knife
- ruler
- fun paper, photos, etc.
- glue
- string or ribbon

(1) Cut the paper into a long rectangle. The book below is 17¾ inches (45 cm) long and 5 inches (13 cm) high.

(2) Decide how many pages the book should have and divide the length of the paper in four, five, six... (however many you'd like) equal sections. Mark where the fold lines should be. It will look like an accordian when folded.

(3) Using the utility knife, lightly trace the fold lines. Alternate between the front and the back—do the front first, then flip the book over and do the same fold line on the back. Repeat for all of the fold lines. **Take note:** Don't cut all the way through the paper! The cuts are just to make folding the zigzag book easier.

(4) Crop the fun paper or photos to match the size of the pages and glue them in. Draw or write something as a caption, tie a nice string or some ribbon around the book, and you're done!

38 WOVEN PAPER

Over, under, over, under... Done!

SUPPLIES
- **drawing paper in various colors**
- **scissors**
- **tape, optional**

(1) Fold a large sheet of drawing paper in half lengthwise and cut equal strips into the folded edge. The lines should end a centimeter or two away from the other edge (just like with the paper lantern on page 134). Open the folded sheet of paper and lay it on the table. This is the loom.

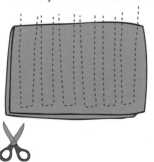

(2) Now cut several strips of equal width, lengthwise, from sheets of different colored paper. This is what you will weave with.

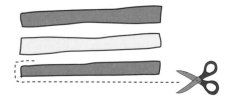

⭐ TIP! Weaving is a great technique for making placemats. Or use the technique to make a colorful blanket to put on the cover of a get-well-soon card for a sick friend (go to page 125, quick!).

(3) Weave the first strip, alternating over then under the strips of the paper loom.

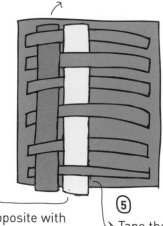

(4) Do the exact opposite with the next strip of paper—weave over first, then under. Shift the strips of paper as close to each other as possible. Keep going until the loom is full.

(5) Tape the ends of the woven strips to the loom t ensure tha they stay i place.

64

39 SUPER-QUICK FINGER CROCHETING

Just like real crocheting, but without the hook.
Perfect for little hands!

SUPPLIES

• wool
• nimble fingers

① Make a loop in the wool.

②

Insert your thumb and index finger in the loop and grab the long end of the wool with these fingers, keeping the loose end to the side.

③

Pull the wool through the first loop until you make another loop. Pull the loop lightly.

④

Repeat. The crocheted garland will keep getting longer.

40 HEAVENLY MOBILE

Ah, crafting with dried pasta... It's been a while!

SUPPLIES

- dried pasta that has a hole in it (e.g. penne)
- blue and white paint and paintbrush
- string
- thick white paper or cardboard
- black felt pen
- hole punch, optional

(1) Paint the pasta in a few different shades of white, light blue, and dark blue. Allow to dry fully.

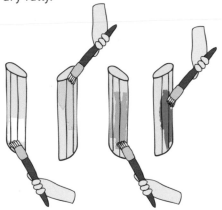

(2) Meanwhile, cut a cloud shape out of thick paper or cardboard. Cut or punch a few holes on the underside.

(3) Thread the pasta onto the string and tie each length, one by one, onto the cloud through the holes you made.

41 TISSUE PAPER ART

If I had a dollar for every bit of tissue paper I've scrunched up and glued onto something, I'd be a millionaire.

SUPPLIES

- **tissue paper in various colors**
- **drawing paper**
- **craft glue**
- **scissors, optional**

①
If you'd like, cut out a paper shape to work with ahead of time.

②
Tear off a piece of tissue paper and scrunch it into a little ball. Glue it wherever you'd like on the paper shape and keep going until the artwork is finished.

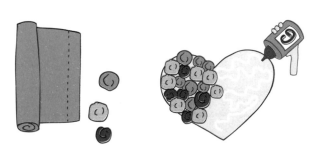

PERFECT PARTIES

Secretly, I like the preparation for parties at least as much as the parties themselves. Inviting people, deciding on food, and stealthily making all the preparations, right up until the big day arrives. Party time!

42 ORIGINAL INVITATIONS

The fun of a party starts with the invitations. So, make them something special!

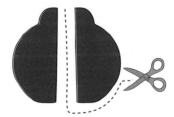

YOU'RE INVITED

LET'S PARTY!

① Draw a large circle in pencil on two sheets of drawing paper by tracing a large plate.

② Draw a smaller half circle on top for the ladybug's head or a long rectangle for the stem of the flower. Cut out the ladybug or flower.

③ Cut the entire top shape in two, lengthwise, through the middle, leaving the shape below intact.

④ Lay the paper pieces on top of each other and press a split pin through them (pre-make the hole using a hole punch, if you'd like). Be sure to overlap the corners of the top piece.

⑤ Finish off the invitation. Draw the dots on the ladybug, for example, and write a message on the inside.

 TIP! True 80s fans really should make a Pac-Man version of the invitation.

43 PIMP YOUR STRAWS

Never accidentally slurp someone else's drink again.

① Think up a funny or appropriate figure or symbol for every guest. Draw the figure, color it in, and glue it on a straw. Or, use the same figure for everyone and write people's names or change the color scheme for each person.

② Let each guest pick out a personalized straw.

⭐ **TIP!** Also fun: Glue crazy mini-photos or drawings of your guests themselves on the straws.

44 PARTY GARLAND

Even more friends to celebrate with—who could say no?

- 1 long, narrow strip of wallpaper or tissue paper
- pencil
- scissors

① Fold the strip of paper into a zigzag form.

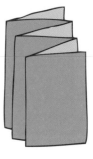

② Using a pencil, draw a figure onto the front of the paper zigzag. Make sure that the hands and feet always touch the folds on the left and right sides.

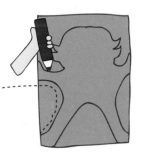

③ Cut out the figure, unfold the garland, and hang it up!

 TIP! For a longer garland, just attach a few together with tape.

45 LIFE-SIZE SIGNPOSTS

My youngest, kindergarten-age daughter made these at school with her teacher. Now her silhouette points the way to the girls' bathroom.

SUPPLIES

- **1 large sheet of drawing paper (or old sheet of wallpaper or a variety of smaller sheets of paper taped together)**
- **paint and paintbrushes**
- **scissors**
- **pencil**
- **a friend**

 Lay the paper on the ground and paint it completely using broad brushstrokes. Allow to dry fully.

② Have one person lie down on top of the painted paper, striking any pose.

③ Using a pencil, have someone else trace the outline of the person lying down on the paper. Cut out the silhouette.

④ Hang the "signpost" on the wall.

46 PARTY PIÑATA

I love piñatas, but I can't stand the giant mess *papier-maché* always ends up being. That's why I'm so happy to present to you one of my favorite crafts: the no-fuss piñata.

SUPPLIES

- **1 empty breakfast cereal box**
- **things for inside the piñata: candy, confetti, etc.**
- **paper (tissue, crepe, or Kraft paper)**
- **glue**
- **tape**
- **string**
- **duct tape**
- **utility knife**
- **black felt pen**
- **stick**
- **feathers, optional**

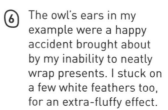

① Fill the cereal box with the prize(s) and tape the box shut. Securely attach the string to the top of the box using duct tape.

② Make several cuts in the bottom of the box using a utility knife to make sure that it doesn't take 312 hours for someone to break the piñata.

③ Wrap the box in paper, just like wrapping a present. Then start decorating.

④ Stick long strips of paper that reach at least around the front and sides of the box onto the box using tape. Cut "tassels" into the strips of paper to make them look more festive. This owl has alternating brown and white strips, but rainbow colors are also an option. As are minions!

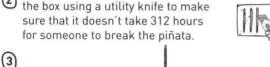

⑤ Cut big eyes out of yellow paper, draw in the pupils using a black felt pen, and glue them on the box. Cut a diamond shape out of black or brown paper for the beak, fold it in half, and glue it on.

⑥ The owl's ears in my example were a happy accident brought about by my inability to neatly wrap presents. I stuck on a few white feathers too, for an extra-fluffy effect.

⑦ Hang the piñata up high and let the kids take turns giving it a whack until it breaks.

47 DANCE POMPOMS

Shake that pompom, baby!

SUPPLIES
- **10 to 12 plastic garbage bags**
- **scissors**
- **duct tape**

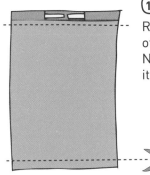

① Rip a garbage bag off the roll, but DO NOT unfurl it. Lay it on the table.

② Cut off the top and bottom. (My garbage bags had a drawstring—I used this yellow string in the pompoms).

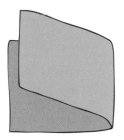

③ Fold the garbage bag in half, widthwise.

④ Cut the plastic into strips (from the open side), staying a few centimeters away from the fold line. Try to keep them all more or less the same length, but it doesn't matter if you make a mistake or two.

⑤ Do the same with the other garbage bags and place them on top of each other, lined up along the fold line.

⑥ Roll the bags into a bundle and secure them in place using duct tape. Now you have a pompom with a handle.

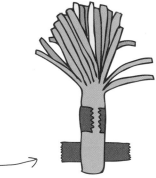

48 CAKE GARLAND

It isn't a party without a cake and it isn't a cake without a mini-garland

SUPPLIES

- paper
- string
- 2 long, wooden skewers
- scissors
- craft glue
- a cake
- marker, optional

① Cut diamond shapes out of the paper. The easiest way to do this is to fold the paper in half, lengthwise, and cut triangles along the fold line. That way the flags will be symmetrical.

② Coat the underside of the diamonds with glue and lay them with the underside of the fold facing the string. Press the diamonds closed so that there's a triangle on either side of the string.

③ When the garland is finished, tie each end to a wooden skewer. Don't make the string longer than the cake. Decorate with faux feathers or mini-balloons.

④ Stick the garland on the cake and...party!

49 DO-IT-YOURSELF DANCE RIBBON

You don't need much to make this dance ribbon. Turn up the volume!

SUPPLIES

- **1 stick**
- **paint and paintbrush**
- **1 long ribbon of crepe paper or fabric**

①
Paint the stick a nice, bright color. Allow to dry fully.

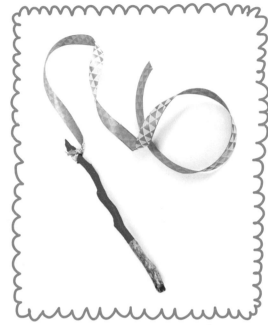

② Tie the ribbon tightly around the end of the stick and...done!

50 MESSAGE IN A BALLOON

Your party is only really complete when everyone gets a balloon to take home at the end. To pop and read your message, of course!

SUPPLIES
- **as many balloons as there are party guests**
- **strips of paper**
- **confetti**
- **permanent pen or markers**

(1) Blow up each balloon and keep it inflated for 30 seconds. Allow the balloon to deflate. It's much easier to fill them this way.

(2) Write a nice personal message on each strip of paper, roll it up as small as possible and insert it into the balloon along with a bunch of confetti. (Use a funnel if this is too difficult.)

(3) Draw something cool or write the name of a guest on each balloon (use a marker that won't run) and hand them out for when the guests leave.

KNOW YOUR
CLASSICS

Chances are good that, at some point, your parents also made a collage, played with a tin-can telephone, or made a magic coin appear with coloring. So why not invite them over next week for a Wednesday afternoon with cake, coffee, and crafts?

51 SCOUBIDOU

The playground trend known as gimp is back!

• **2 plastic gimp threads**

① Hook the threads onto each other.

A   C

B   D

② Place the lowermost thread on the right (D) on top of the uppermost thread on the right (C).

③ Place the uppermost thread on the left (A) on top of the lowermost thread on the left (B).

④ Take thread B and thread it through the loop on the right.

⑤ Now take thread C and thread it through the loop on the left.

⑥ Pull the threads tightly to form a knot.

⑦ Hold the knot in place with your index finger and lay the lowermost thread on the right over top of the thread above. Then, lay the uppermost thread on the left over the thread underneath.

⑧ Pull the other two threads through the loops that have been created on the opposite side, following the arrows in the image.

⑨ Repeat steps 7 and 8 until your scoubidou is finished.

★ **TIP!** Once you figure out this basic square knotting technique, the variations are endless! The Internet is your friend.

82

52 ACCORDION FOLDING

Accordion folding—so that's what this is called!

SUPPLIES

- **2 thin strips of paper in the same or different colors**
- **glue or tape**

(1) Place the two ends of the strips of paper on top of one another so that they form a right angle. Glue them in place.

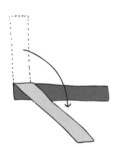

(2) Now fold the bottom strip straight over the top one. The strips of paper should stay in a right angle.

(3) Do the same with the other strip of paper and repeat until all of the paper is used up and you've made an accordion shape.

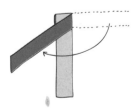

⭐ Use the accordion folds as arms and legs for a person, as tentacles for
TIP! an octopus, or use them to make a surprise "jump" out of a closed box.

53 FORK POMPOMS

Dress up a gift or your hat. Add it to a sock puppet or a garland. Pompoms are good for just about anything. They're also super quick to make.

SUPPLIES
- **fork with 4 tines**
- **yarn**
- **small scissors**

① Wrap the yarn around the tines of the fork a few times, keeping the loose end on the side and wrapping the yarn around it so that it stays in place. The more times the yarn is wrapped around the fork, the thicker the pompom will be; however, the risk that the pompom won't stay together also increases. It's a matter of finding the happy medium between fluffy and securely bound.

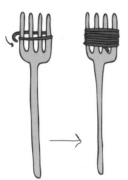

② Thread a shorter piece of the same yarn through the middle of the tines of the fork and tie the bundle of yarn together tightly in a double knot.

③ Carefully slide the bundle of yarn off the fork.

④ Cut the loops of yarn apart on both sides. Trim any uneven bits off with scissors until it's nice and round and carefully open up the pompom.

★ TIP! To make a larger pompom, use the classic technique that relies on a cardboard disc.

54 MAGIC COINS

A president's head or the grand bald eagle—which will end up on your paper? Drawing them are a snap using this amazing technique.

SUPPLIES
- coins
- paper
- pencil

① Place a coin on the table.

② Lay a sheet of paper over the top of the coin. Hold the sheet of paper in place so that the coin stays put.

③ Rub the pencil over the paper where it covers the coin. Don't press too hard, but don't press too softly either.

④ Slowly but surely, the imprint of the coin will appear on the paper. Magic!

★ Give this technique a try with a
TIP! tree leaf instead of a coin.

55 TIN CAN TELEPHONE

"Hello? Yes? I'd like to order two well-behaved children, please."
"Okay! They'll be there soon."

SUPPLIES

- **2 empty, clean tin cans**
- **1 long piece of string**
- **nail**
- **hammer**

①
Hammer the nail into the bottom of each can and then remove it.

② Thread the string through each hole and tie it in place with a sturdy knot on the inside of the cans.

③
Give each child a can and have them stand as far apart as possible so that the string is taut. Taut string = good reception. One person talks into a can while the other person holds a can up to his or her ear.

⭐ Take note: The inside edges of tin cans can be very sharp.
TIP! Cover the edges with tape or sand the inside so it's smooth.

56 BLOWN TREES

Remember that moment when you discovered you could blow ink trees and branches through your straw? I do! (It was a Saturday morning, during a drawing lesson.)

SUPPLIES
- **smooth drawing paper**
- **India ink or Chinese ink**
- **straw**
- **paintbrush**

①

On the paper, paint a thick tree trunk using the paintbrush.

②

Let a drop of ink fall on the top of the tree trunk. Blow the drop upward using the straw. Continue to blow small drops of ink away from the trunk to make more and more branches until you have a fully-formed tree.

③

Make several trees alongside each other to create a real landscape. The branches can definitely be craggy in terms of shape—that's how they are in nature, too, just take a look.

★ Once the ink has dried, use a cotton swab or a fine paintbrush to paint buds on the
TIP! branches. Pink blossoms on the branches will turn the tree into a Japanese cherry.

57 OOH LA LA: COLLAGE

When you don't feel like getting into anything complicated. When you're looking to get rid of a pile of old magazines. When you want to transform all the bad news in the paper into something happy. Then it's high time for a collage!

SUPPLIES

- old newspapers and magazines
- drawing paper
- scissors
- glue

①

You really can't do anything wrong when you're making a collage. Ripping or cutting? A face, landscape, or something abstract? Working only with black and white newspaper clippings, or certain shades of colors? Or only cutting out real shapes like eyes, hands, or vegetables? And drawing something yourself as well? If you consult the dictionary, a collage is a whole made up of various parts that are stuck together, which means that anything is possible and everything is allowed!

★ For younger children, it can be helpful to have them (or help them)
TIP! draw a sort of guide in pencil first, like a tree, a sun, or a hilltop.

58 POPCORN PARTY

For a party that pops.

SUPPLIES

- **popcorn kernels**
- **coffee filters**
- **powdered sugar or salt**
- **marker**

①
Make the popcorn according to the package instructions.

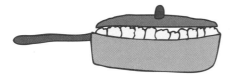

②
Write a funny message or the name of guests on the coffee filters.

③
Serve the popcorn in the coffee filters. Sprinkle with powdered sugar or salt, to taste.

SUNNY SUMMER

Oh, how summer vacations used to feel endlessly long! One small problem: When the weather doesn't allow for playing or swimming outside, it's only a matter of time before you'll hear the phrase feared by parents the world over—"Mom, Dad, I'm bored!" The next time you find yourself in that situation, simply turn to these pages.

59 PIMPED CANS

Is your desk covered with a bunch of stuff from the school year that just ended? Start your summer vacation with some tidying up—made much easier with these fun storage containers.

- empty, clean tin cans
- decorations: yarn, washi tape, fabric, paper, adhesive film, ribbon, etc.
- glue

There are so many ways to give a can a makeover:

- Cut fabric, paper, or adhesive film to size and stick it on the can. Finish with a decorative ribbon around the top.

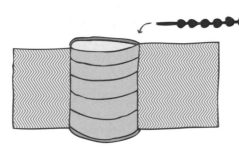

- Make a composition with washi tape.

- Cover the can with glue and tightly wind yarn or string around the can.

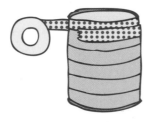

⭐ Take note: The inside edges of tin cans can be very sharp.
TIP! Cover the edges with tape or sand the inside so it's smooth.

60 CRAZY CATAPULT

How. Cool. Is. This.

SUPPLIES

- a few wooden popsicle sticks
- 4 elastic bands
- 1 small lid (e.g. from medicine or a plastic bottle)
- 1 small ball (or cotton ball, pompom, etc.)
- 1 split pin
- hole punch, scissors, or knife, optional

① Stack a few wooden popsicle sticks on top of each other. (Not too high, because then it won't work as well.)

② Wind an elastic band around each side. Make it nice and tight!

③ Place one stick on top, perpendicular to the stack of sticks, and another one on the bottom parallel to the first. Fasten these in place by wrapping an elastic in an *X* shape around the sticks.

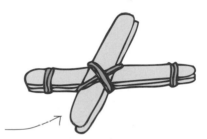

④ Tightly wrap another elastic around the two sticks on one side.

⑤ Finally, attach the lid to the end of the uppermost stick. You can do this using glue (but in our experience this makes the catapult less durable). A more robust version can be made by making a small hole in the uppermost stick and the lid with a hole punch or a knife, and pushing a split pin through them both.

⑥ Place the ball in the lid, push the stick down, and let it fly!

 TIP! It's also sooo much fun to use your catapult for target practice—by hanging up a bullseye with points on the wall. All the players stand in a row with their catapults. Who will get the highest score?

61 UFOs

Beam me up, Scotty!

SUPPLIES
- drawing paper
- 2 transparent plastic cups
- washi tape
- 2 paper plates
- scissors
- glue
- markers
- aluminum foil, optional
- straws or string, optional

① Draw a Martian on a sheet of paper and cut it out. Make sure it fits inside the plastic cup.

② Tape the paper plates together, with the rounded side facing outward. If you'd like, you can cover the paper plates with aluminum foil.

③ Turn the plastic cups upside down. Attach one to the bottom of the UFO (with its opening facing down). Place your Martian in the other cup before attaching it to the top.

④ You can stand your UFO up, supported by a few straws, or you can hang it up using a bit of string.

62 FUNNY ROBOT

Did I mention that cardboard boxes are worth their weight in gold? You can't go wrong with a cardboard robot. Really make it your own.

- **cardboard boxes**
- **markers**
- **large, flexible tubing (e.g. flexible duct hose)**
- **utility knife**
- **string**
- **pipe cleaners, cotton balls, and aluminum foil, optional, for antennae**

①

Make the body first. For this version, I used a sheet of cardboard for the belly because it appears that walking around the house wearing a cardboard box is moderately to very inconvenient. I used the handle that was already cut into the box as the on/off switch to activate the robot.

②

For the head, take a box and cut two holes for the eyes. Insert a pipe cleaner into the top and affix balls of aluminum foil to the ends.

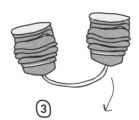

③

Connect two pieces of flexible tubing with string. This way you can put them on like a tubing-sleeve jacket.

63 THE SCREAM

My daughters' school ran a two-week-long art project last year and the whole school was transformed into a museum! I secretly stole this painting and took it home with me.

- black and white photo of your child re-enacting *The Scream* (show the real thing first as an example and you'll score some extra points in the area of art education)
- thick paper, at least A3 size (11" x 17", 297 x 420 mm) or larger
- paint and paintbrushes
- glue

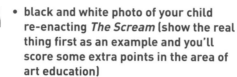

① Cut the photo out around the edges of the silhouette.

② Paint the sheet of paper by copying the background of the original. Keep it simple for smaller children— green, blue, and shades of orange on top.

③ Glue the cut-out photo onto the right spot and the artwork will be museum ready!

64 SUPER-QUICK SQUID

A super-quick squid? You can make one in no time.

- **1 toilet paper roll**
- **scissors**
- **paint and paintbrush or markers**
- **googly eyes**

① Cut the squid's tentacles. You do this by making eight more or less equal cuts, ¾ to 1 inch (2 to 3 cm) deep, into the bottom of the toilet paper roll.

② Paint or color the roll. (This is easiest if you insert your index and middle fingers into the roll and spread them apart, while holding the paintbrush with your other hand.)

③ Allow to dry.

④ Stick the googly eyes onto the squid and spread out its tentacles.

65 MARBLE TRACK

Just bought the perfect pair of boots? Make sure you keep the box—you'll have yourself a marble track too!

SUPPLIES
- **large shoebox**
- **wooden craft sticks**
- **utility knife**
- **ping pong ball or marble**
- **marker**
- **paint, optional**

① If you want to paint the box, do it first. I used leftover fluorescent pink spray paint.

② Make a variety of cuts using a utility knife. Make sure that the cuts are as wide as the wooden sticks. Also, ensure that the marble or ball can actually reach the bottom of the track. Alternate between horizontal and vertical cuts.

③ Insert a wooden stick into every cut.

④ In some places, you can insert several sticks together so that you create a sort of basket for your ball to land in. Assign a certain number of points to each basket.

⑤ Hold the box flat with both hand and roll the ball slowly back and forth. Can you get the ball in all of the baskets?

66 TWISTED-PAPER CATERPILLAR

A small but fun craft. Sometimes it doesn't need to be any more complicated than that.

SUPPLIES

- **paper in various colors**
- **scissors**
- **tape or glue**
- **googly eyes, optional**

① Make a paper chain, as seen on page 21.

② Cut a large teardrop shape out of paper for the caterpillar's head. Glue or tape this, upside down, onto the first ring of the paper chain. Cut out two antennae as well and attach them to the head.

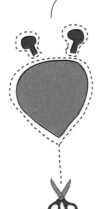

③ Stick or draw eyes and a mouth on your caterpillar.

67 FRIENDSHIP BRACELET

If you and your best friend both wear the same friendship bracelet, then you really are BFFs. Wow!

SUPPLIES

- **6 lengths of embroidery thread, 35 inches (90 cm) long, 2 of each color**
- **tape**
- **scissors**
- **1 bead, optional**

1. Put the threads together, color by color, make a loop at the top, and tie it off with a double knot. Tape the loop to the table—it makes things easier.

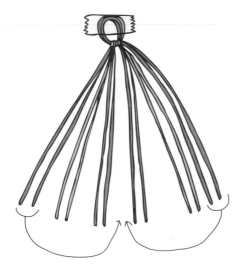

3. When the bracelet is long enough, tie it off with a double knot. You can also string a bead on the end and tie another double knot to hold it in place. To put the bracelet on and take it off, simply thread the bead through the loop made in the beginning. (Otherwise, you'll have to cut the bracelet off.)

2. Take the two outermost threads on the right side and lay them on top of the four other threads on the right. Now take the two outermost threads on the left side and lay them on top of the four other threads on the left and cross over the two innermost threads on the right in such a way that you make an *X* in the middle. Pull tightly in place. Repeat this with the outside threads until the bracelet is long enough.

68 PUFFY BALLOON ANIMALS

Balloons are always a hit, but if you turn them into funny animals, you'll really have a number one hit.

SUPPLIES

- **balloons in various colors**
- **drawing paper in various colors**
- **permanent, waterproof marker**
- **scissors**
- **glue**
- **tape, optional**

① Blow up the balloon and tie it closed.

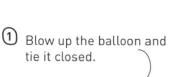

② Cut ears, fins, or paws out of paper and attach them to the balloon.

③ Draw a nice or naughty face on the balloon.

69 PAPER FLOWERS

Who wants to buy a flower in exchange for seven shells?

SUPPLIES
- **tissue paper in various colors**
- **wooden skewer**
- **scissors**
- **tape**
- **thin wire**

(1) Cut a thin strip of green tissue paper and wrap it around the wooden skewer. Affix the end with tape. Now you have your stem.

(2) Cut about eight sheets of tissue paper that are 6" x 12" (15 x 30 cm) each. The longer your sheet of paper, the bigger your flower.

(3) Neatly arrange the sheets on top of each other and fold them into a zigzag shape.

(4) Wrap a piece of wire around the middle of the folded tissue paper.

(5) Carefully open the sheets of paper to reveal a full, beautiful flower. Trim any uneven bits.

(6) Twist the wire around the stem and you're ready to go!

70 NINJAAAS!

These ninjas are officially the coolest little guys in this book.

SUPPLIES

- 1 brown paper bag
- thick colored paper
- scissors
- glue
- 4 split pins
- marker or googly eyes

① Place the bag on the table with the opening facing you. If the top is already folded, you can start right away. If not, fold the end of the bag toward you.

② Measure the dimensions of your ninja's belly and cut a piece of drawing paper to size. Glue it onto the belly.

③ Stick or draw eyes onto the folded section of the bag, at the top.

④ Cut four strips of colored drawing paper, two for the arms and two for the legs. The strips for the legs should be a tiny bit longer than those for the arms.

⑤ Measure two strips of different colored drawing paper and cut them out. These will be the bands above and below the ninja's eyes. Glue them in place.

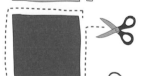

⑥ Attach the arms and the legs to the ninja's belly. In order to do this, poke small holes where the split pins will be. That way it'll be easier to insert them. But take note: Don't push the split pins all the way through the back of paper bag. By affixing them to the belly only, you'll have more room for your hand inside the bag.

71 MAGIC SAND

Has bad weather ruled out the sandbox? Just bring the sandbox inside, right? Okay, a slightly less messy version then.

SUPPLIES

- **8 cups (1 kg) flour**
- **1 cup (235 ml) baby oil**
- **sand toys or jars and empty bottles**

(1) Mix the flour and oil thoroughly in a large bowl. Magic cake, anyone?

72 LUCKY CARP

In Japan, these carp-shaped *koinobori* windsocks are hung up on Children's Day. But around here, every day is children's day, isn't it?

SUPPLIES

- 1 toilet paper roll
- string
- 1 bamboo stake
- tissue paper
- googly eyes
- glue
- scissors

① On the front end of the toilet paper roll, make two holes opposite each other and then thread the string through those holes, tying the loose end to the bamboo stake.

② Cut out circles of tissue paper, fold them in half, and glue them to the toilet paper roll. These are the fish's scales.

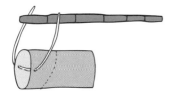

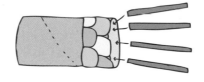

③ For the tail, cut out several long strips of tissue paper and glue them to the inside of the toilet paper roll, all the way around, on the back end.

④ Stick the eyes onto the front end.

73 MONDRIAAN WITH TAPE

Thumbs up for artwork that's truly wall ready.

SUPPLIES

- **thick, white paper or a canvas**
- **red, blue, yellow, and black paint**
- **paintbrush**
- **thin masking tape or washi tape**

① Stick the tape onto the canvas or paper in straight lines to divide up the surface into squares and rectangles of varying sizes. Have a look at a real Mondriaan painting for inspiration.

③ Let the paint dry completely and then carefully remove the tape.

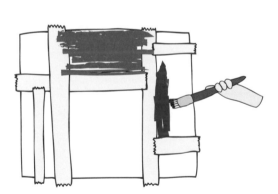

② Decide which areas should be red, yellow, blue, black, or white. For younger children, it can be helpful to paint a dot of the color in each area to guide them. Paint all of the squares/rectangles.

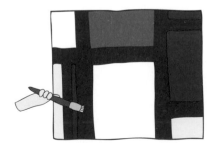

④ Color or paint black the lines that appear from under the tape.

KNOW YOUR
CLASSICS

Even in the summer, whether we like it or not, it can sometimes end up being crafting weather. It's even more fun, though, when you can move the entire crafting table outside. Sitting together, under an umbrella, no whining about the mess, and a few classics in the making... Super summery!

74 HAPPY BOOKMARKS

This one goes way, way back. A tried-and-true Mother's or Father's Day gift: the handy bookmark. But you've never seen one this original before.

(1) Laminate the photo or glue it to sturdy paper.

(2) Cut out the figure, neatly, along the edges.

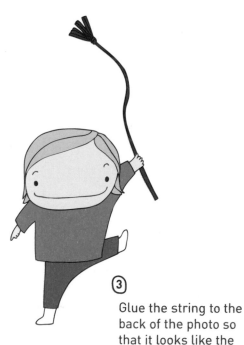

(3) Glue the string to the back of the photo so that it looks like the child is holding it.

75 PINWHEEL

Beautiful and environmentally friendly.

SUPPLIES

- **colored drawing paper**
- **pencil and ruler**
- **utility knife**
- **scissors**
- **markers or paint**
- **glue**
- **straight pin**
- **bead**
- **bamboo or other kind of stick**
- **hammer and nail**

① Cut a square from the sheet of paper. Ours was 7" x 7" (18 x 18 cm), but yours can be bigger or smaller.

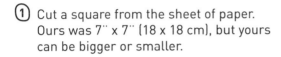

② Use the ruler to draw two straight lines on the square, intersecting in the middle to divide the square into four equal areas. Color or paint each of these, or glue a square of paper onto them. Allow to dry fully.

③ Draw two diagonal lines on the square. Cut along these diagonal lines, avoiding the middle by about 1 inch (3 cm) on each side.

④ Fold the second triangle at every corner toward the middle. Don't let the points overlap. Insert the straight pin through the four corners from front to back. Push the bead onto the pin so that the pinwheel can spin more easily later.

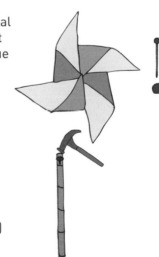

⑤ Use the hammer and nail to make a hole in the stick. Remove the nail and attach the pinwheel to the stick with the straight pin.

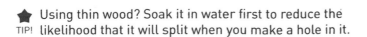

★ Using thin wood? Soak it in water first to reduce the
TIP! likelihood that it will split when you make a hole in it.

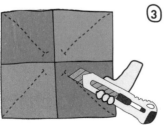

76 MULTICOLORED SALT

The classic to end all classics!

- lots of table salt
- flat plate or a large sheet of paper
- colored chalk
- empty glass jars with lids
- funnel (or a sheet of paper you can roll into a cone shape)
- long wooden skewers, optional

① Pour a bunch of salt onto the plate or large sheet of paper. (Paper makes it easier to transfer the salt to the jars).

② Place a piece of chalk flat on top of the salt and roll it back and forth until the salt becomes the desired color. The longer you roll, the deeper the color will be.

③ Pour the colored salt into a jar using the funnel or a paper cone.

④ Good tricks that have an instant effect:

Make the colors of the rainbow.

Insert a wooden skewer along the inside of the jar to create depth in your salt art.

Use different shades of blue—with wooden skewer waves! And what about a mini-boat made of paper for the top of your "sea" (see the next page) or some of your best shells.

77 PAPER BOAT

If you can fold a paper hat, then a boat isn't very far off.

SUPPLIES

- **sheet of paper or old newspaper**

① Make a paper hat (see page 18) and place it in front of you with the opening facing down.

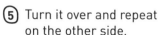

② Fold both of the corners of the rim of the hat together, over the edge so you're left with a triangle.

③ Stick your thumbs into the hat and pull the paper open so it becomes a flat diamond shape.

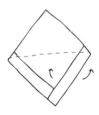

④ Fold the lower flap up, toward the top, even with the uppermost point of the diamond.

⑤ Turn it over and repeat on the other side.

⑥ Stick your thumbs in the paper again and make another diamond shape.

⑦ Pull the uppermost point of the diamond apart and your boat is done!

The Terrible Story of the Capsized Captain

Tell this story the next time you fold a paper boat. Wide eyes and open mouths guaranteed!

There was once a captain who sailed over the Paper Sea. One day, there was a terrible storm, the kind with lightning strikes so fierce that they make your hair stand on end and with so much rain that you are soaked down to your underwear. It was too much for the captain's ship—the mast came crashing down. (Rip the top of the inside triangle off.)

Then the front of the ship hit a gigantic rock, BOOM! The captain ran to the bow of the ship, but it had broken off completely. (Rip one side of the boat off.) Right after, the captain heard a loud thwack as the ship's stern was also hit. (Rip the other side of the boat off.)

The ship sank with everyone aboard. The only thing that was found was the captain's t-shirt that had washed ashore. (Unfold to reveal a t-shirt.)

78 ANTI-STRESS BALL

Great for releasing some negative energy.
(This is also great for grown-ups.)

SUPPLIES
- **1 balloon**
- **fine-grain filling (e.g. sand, rice, couscous, or cornstarch)**
- **funnel**
- **waterproof marker**

① Blow up the balloon, keep it inflated for 30 seconds, and then release the air.

② Insert the funnel into the balloon's opening and hold it tightly with one hand. With the other hand, pour the filling into the balloon, bit by bit. The balloon shouldn't be filled completely; the ball should be about the size of the palm of your hand.

③ Tie the balloon closed.

④ Draw a funny, angry, or anxious face on the anti-stress ball.

79 QUICK SOCK PUPPET

Because, for some unknown reason, there's always a few lonely socks that manage to escape the washing machine. Because there are holes in your socks and you're not into darning. The perfect excuse to buy new socks: Make a sock puppet out of your old ones!

SUPPLIES

- **old sock**
- **felt or fabric remnants**
- **craft glue or all-purpose glue**
- **2 googly eyes or cotton balls**
- **wool remnants**
- **scissors**
- **marker, optional**
- **needle and thread, optional**

① Put one hand in the sock and mark where the mouth and eyes should be.

② Cut a piece of felt or fabric in a diamond shape or circle and glue it in place where the mouth should be. Want to attach it more securely? Sew the fabric in place with a needle and thread.

③ Glue or sew the eyes on top of the head. If using cotton balls, draw the pupils on.

④ Decorate the puppet with hair made of wool or pompoms or whatever is on hand!

 TIP! For younger kids, it's helpful to insert a tennis ball in the sock before decorating it, or staple a bit of cardboard inside for more support.

80 TIN CAN TOSS GAME

Hello, county fair!

SUPPLIES
- at least 6 empty, clean tin cans
- drawing paper
- black marker
- craft glue
- ball
- scissors

①

Draw funny faces (or numbers 1 to 6) on a sheet of paper.

② Cut the faces out and glue them onto the cans.

③

Stack the cans on top of each other. Who can knock them all down?

⭐ **TIP!** Take note: The inside edges of tin cans can be very sharp. Cover the edges with tape or sand or file the inside so it's smooth.

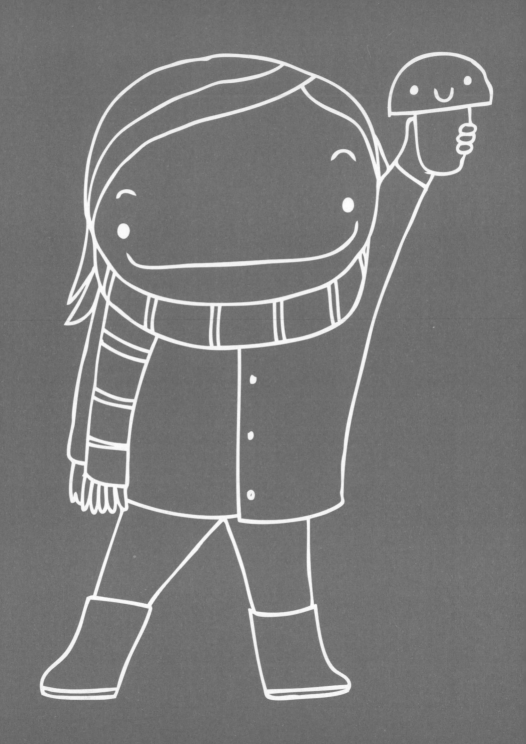

FABULOUS FALL

When autumn arrives, many people experience a strong need for a nose full of forest air. Go together to search for toadstools, gnomes, walking sticks, and leaves in all the colors of the rainbow. Then head back inside with rosy cheeks, a cup of soup in hand, and your crafting gear within reach.

81 HANDPRINT PAINTING

What's better than messing around in paint with your bare hands?

SUPPLIES

- paint in fall colors
- paintbrush
- drawing paper

① Paint the entire palm of your hand and the underside of your wrist brown. Spread your fingers wide and press your hand onto the paper. This will make the trunk of the tree and its branches. Add a bit more paint where necessary.

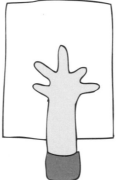

② Wash and dry your hands. Now use your fingertips to make fall leaves in a variety of colors. Don't forget the leaves that have already fallen onto the ground!

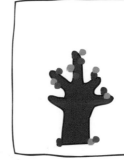

82 FALL PHANTOMS

Get instant spooky ambiance in your house with these creepy scenes.

SUPPLIES

- paper plates
- orange paint (or yellow and red)
- paintbrush
- black paper
- scissors
- glue

① Paint the matte side of the paper plates orange, like the evening sky. Allow to dry fully.

② Meanwhile, cut out all manner of creepy phantoms: a bat, a witch, a lightning bolt, or a jack-o'-lantern.

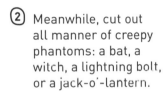

③ Arrange the phantoms on the painted plate and glue them down.

83 HAPPY FOX

This one is really a piece of cake. Plus, there's a bonus! You get to take an autumn walk first!

SUPPLIES

- **1 large fall leaf**
- **white paper**
- **scissors**
- **black marker**
- **glue**
- **pompom, optional**

①

Place the leaf in front you, with the stem pointing up.

③

Glue the eyes onto the leaf and glue a pompom on for the nose.

②

Cut two circles out of the paper and draw pupils on them for the eyes.

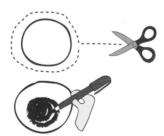

84 MAKE-YOUR-OWN PUZZLE

Who will be the puzzle champion?

SUPPLIES

- **drawing paper**
- **drawing or painting supplies**
- **cardboard**
- **utility knife**
- **ruler**
- **glue, optional**

①

Draw or paint a picture. If the paper used is thin, glue the artwork onto a piece of sturdy cardboard first and allow to dry fully.

② Cut up the drawing or painting into pieces. This can be done any way—in crazy shapes or nice neat rows. The younger the puzzler, the bigger the pieces should be.

③ Mark each of the four corners to give an idea of where to begin putting the puzzle together.

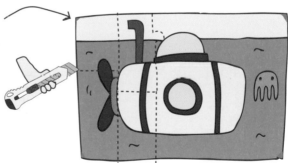

④

You can also print out a photo of the completed puzzle onto cardstock if you like to work with an example.

85 NATURE ART

In the forest, all the craft material you could ever want is just laying at you feet—and it doesn't cost anything! When you get home, you can get to wor on your crafting, with a bowl of the freshly cracked nuts you just collected

- **photo of your child (in a surprised position/with a surprised expression)**
- **scissors**
- **forest materials: branches, leaves, nutshells, etc. (don't forget a bag if you're heading out to collect items)**
- **glue**
- **cardboard, canvas, or thick paper**
- **paint, optional**

① If you'd like, paint a background for the forest scene.

② Cut out the photo along the edges and glue it near the bottom of the paper/canvas.

③

Glue the forest materials here and there. It will look like your tiny child is wandering around in a forest full of gigantic leaves.

86 GET-WELL-SOON CARD

Because autumn = runny noses.

SUPPLIES

- cardstock paper
- black-and-white photo of the sick person
- scissors
- glue
- markers

① Fold your piece of paper in half to make a greeting card.

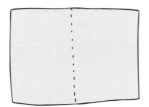

③ Weave a little paper blanket (see page 64) and glue it on top of the photo.

② Cut out the photo along the edges of the person and glue it onto the front of the card.

④ Write a nice message on your card and send it to the person who is sick.

87 AWESOME WALKING STICK

With a walking stick that's as cool as this one, even the most inexperienced hiker will look like a pro.

SUPPLIES
- **strong walking stick**
- **string or wool**
- **paint and paintbrush**
- **extra decorations, optional**

① Paint the stick in bright colors.

② Wrap a piece of wool or string around the stick in a few different places.

③ Dress up the walking stick even more with extra accessories like a found pinecone or feathers.

④ Time to head to the forest!

88 FALL LION

No need to be afraid of this fall lion. The cuteness quotient here is high!

SUPPLIES

- paper plate
- lots of fall leaves (e.g. maple leaves)
- colored pencils, crayons, or paint
- black marker
- glue

① Color the paper plate lion colors (yellow, orange, brown). Draw a face on top using the marker.

② Glue the fall leaves around the outside of the plate to make a real lion's mane.

⭐ **TIP!** A cool (but more complicated) variation is a lion with moving eyes. To make it, cut out the lion's eyes from the plate. Draw eyes on a long strip of paper and tape it to the back of the plate. Don't attach the strip of paper completely, that way you can move the eyes back and forth.

KNOW YOUR
CLASSICS

Crafting makes you hungry!
Thankfully we have the cookies for
any season—they taste good all
year round. Gobble them up in your
cool cardboard castle. Or share
them with your marionette dog?
And then, it's off to dreamland.

89 COOL CARDBOARD CASTLE

Lords and ladies, attention!

SUPPLIES

- **the largest cardboard box you can find**
- **utility knife or scissors**
- **strong string**
- **drawing paper**
- **big sponge**
- **paint**

(1) Choose the best side of the box for the drawbridge. In order to make the drawbridge, position the box with the opening facing up and cut open the left and right sides of one side of the box.

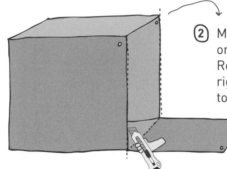

(2) Make two holes, left and right, on the drawbridge itself. Repeat this on the left and right sides of the castle next to the drawbridge.

(3) Cut two pieces of string and tie them to the castle and the drawbridge on each side.

Cut the battlements out of cardboard remnants and affix (4) them to the top of the castle.

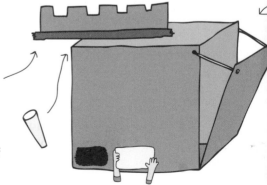

(5) Attach two narrow containers to the rearmost corners of the castle to hold the castle's flags with its shield displayed (a stick with a piece of paper attached to it).

(6) Paint the walls of the castle with a brick pattern by "stamping" the sides with a large sponge dipped in paint.

90 MARIONETTE DOG

Woof!

SUPPLIES

- 2 toilet paper rolls
- 2 craft sticks
- string
- 2 flexible straws
- 2 googly eyes
- scissors
- glue
- hole punch
- paint and paintbrush, optional

(1) Paint the toilet paper rolls as well as the popsicle sticks, if you'd like, in a fun color. Allow to dry.

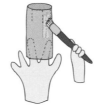

(2) Take one toilet paper roll and cut it in half. One half will be the head. Cut the other half into a stretched-out, figure-8 shape to make the dog's ears.

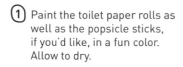

(3) Glue the ears to the top of the head. Push the head down a bit, in between the ears. This way the ears will stick up in a funny way.

(4) Glue the popsicle sticks together in an *X* form.

(5) Now make two holes in the top of the dog's body, one at the front and one at the back. Make holes in the head too, one underneath and one on top, in between the ears.

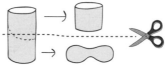

(9) Thread a long piece of string through the head and the body of the dog and tie the end of the string to the wooden, popsicle-stick cross.

(6) Make four small holes lengthwise in the bottom of the other toilet paper roll using the hole punch. The dog's legs will fit into these holes.

(10) Stick the eyes onto the head, glue the flexible part of the straw to the end of the body to make a tail, and...go for a walk!

(8) Cut four straight pieces of straw and thread each one onto each of the dog's string legs, tying the end of the string with a knot to secure the straw.

(7) Thread one piece of string through the back two holes and another through the front two holes.

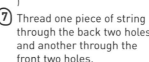

91 DREAMCATCHER

A dreamcatcher traps all of your bad dreams in its net. Only good dreams make it through! If that's not worth trying, I don't know what is.

- **3 sticks or branches**
- **fine string or wool**
- **decorations: feathers, beads, charms, souvenirs, worry dolls, etc.**
- **glue, optional**

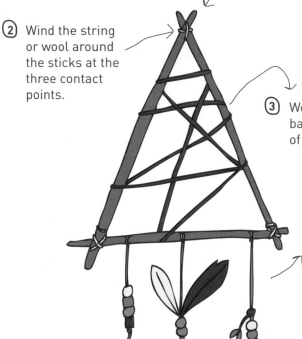

① Lay the sticks on top of each other to form a triangle. You can glue them together for increased durability.

② Wind the string or wool around the sticks at the three contact points.

③ Weave the string or wool back and forth on the inside of the triangle.

④ Tie on the decorations with thread on the lowest stick.

⑤ Hang the dreamcatcher by your bed and have a good sleep!

92 MOOD PLATE

Hang this plate on your bedroom door, give one to every member of your household, or keep them in the kitchen. That way, you'll know who got out of the wrong (or right) side of their bed before you even reach the breakfast table.

SUPPLIES

- **cardstock or cardboard in different colors or patterns**
- **6 split pins**
- **scissors**
- **marker**
- **glue, optional**

(1) If you are going to use paper with a nice pattern, glue it to a sheet of sturdier paper first.

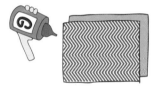

(2) Cut out two eyes, a nose, two cheeks, two rectangles for the eyebrows, and a half circle for the mouth and affix these to the paper or cardboard with split pins.

(3) Turn the shapes to reflect your mood.

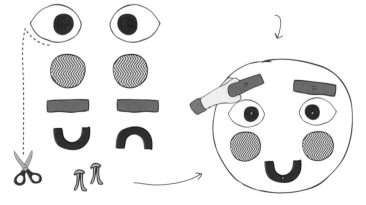

93 PAPER LANTERN

In the winter near the window or in the summer on the patio, lanterns always have a fairy tale–like effect.

SUPPLIES
- 1 sheet of colored paper
- 1 tea light
- 1 small glass jar (without lid)
- scissors
- glue, tape, or stapler

① Fold the sheet of paper in half lengthwise.

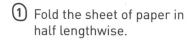

② Cut the paper in equal intervals along the fold line. Stop cutting a few centimeters away from the edge of the paper. Draw a guideline if it helps avoid cutting too far.

③ Unfold the paper and connect the two ends to each other to form a cylinder. Glue or staple the cylinder shut.

④ Light a tea light, place it in the jar, and place the jar in the lantern.

94 COOKIES FOR ANY SEASON

Sometimes, there's nothing kids want more than to bake cookies. This recipe is tasty, easy, and quick. And the delicious cookie smell throughout your house is free of charge.

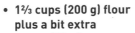

SUPPLIES

- 1⅔ cups (200 g) flour plus a bit extra
- ⅓ cup (75 g) granulated sugar
- 1 teaspoon lemon zest
- pinch of cinnamon
- pinch of salt
- 1 egg
- ½ cup (1 stick or 100 g) cold butter
- 1 cup (120 g) confectioner's sugar
- ½ teaspoon vanilla extract
- 1 to 2 tablespoons (15 to 30 ml) milk
- cookie cutters
- piping bag or plastic freezer bag

① Preheat your oven to 390°F (200°C).

② Combine the flour, sugar, lemon zest, cinnamon, and salt in a mixing bowl.

③ Crack the egg into the mixture.

④ Cut the butter into cubes and add these to the bowl. Knead the mixture together.

⑤ Make a sturdy dough ball and leave it to sit for at least 30 minutes in the fridge.

⑥ Sprinkle your work surface with flour and roll out the dough with a rolling pin.

⑦ Cut shapes out of the dough. Don't have cookie cutters? An upside-down glass works just as well!

⑧ Transfer the cookies to a baking sheet and bake for about 12 minutes until golden brown. Allow to cool fully.

⑨ Meanwhile, mix the confectioner's sugar, vanilla extract, and milk in a bowl. What you're looking for is a thick glaze that's still a bit runny.

⑩ If you don't have a piping bag, transfer the glaze to a plastic freezer bag and cut off one of the bottom corners. Twist the bag closed and draw figures on your cookies. Let the glaze harden and then...attack!

CREEPY
CRAFTING

Woooooo! Creepy things are always fun, but they're extra exciting at the end of the year, when it gets darker earlier outside. Walks by flashlight! Halloween parties! And, the icing on the cake, the most impressive craft in this book to close things off: the deranged dragon.

95 MEXICAN MASK

In Mexico, the *día de los Muertos*, or "day of the dead," is a big deal. People gather at the cemetery, decorate the graves, and make figures and masks with brightly colored skulls.

- **paper plate**
- **thick, black marker**
- **felt pens in bright colors**
- **scissors**

① Cut a curved line into both sides of the lower half of the paper plate. Avoid cutting further than the innermost circle to achieve the best effect.

③ Color in your shapes with the brightly colored felt pens. Done!

② Cut the eyes out, too. Use the black marker to make line drawings. First draw an outline around the entire mask and then around the eyes and above them, for example. You can draw an upside-down heart as a nose, flowers, dots, anything you want.

96 FIRE-BREATHING MONSTER

Some cardboard and a few split pins. You don't need much more than that to make the scariest monster on the block.

SUPPLIES

- **An empty cereal box**
- **scissors or utility knife**
- **10 split pins**
- **glue**
- **ruler, optional**
- **googly eyes, optional**
- **markers or paint, optional**

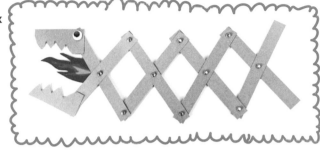

① Cut eight equal-sized strips out of the cereal box cardboard. In our example, the pieces are 6 inches (16 cm) long and ¾ inch (2 cm) wide. Keep three sheets of cardboard aside for the head and the fire.

② Lay the strips of cardboard down, two on top of each other, making an *X* form. Insert a split pin in the middle of each *X* and open the "legs" of the split pin on the back. If you do this with all the pieces of cardboard, you'll have four crosses.

③ Now attach the crosses to each other with split pins. Do this by placing an *X* in front of you and laying down another *X* beside and slightly overlapping the first so that the right side of the first is covered by the left side of the second. Insert split pins on the top and bottom legs to attach the pieces together. Continue until all four crosses are attached this way.

④ Cut fearsome jaws with plenty of sharp teeth out of two pieces of cardboard and glue these to the right-hand side of the monster, one half on top and the other on the bottom.

⑤ Cut the shape of a flame out of cardboard as well. Color or paint it fiery colors and attach it to the middle split pin on the right-hand side.

⑥ Now just add an eye to the top of its head and...take a bite!

⭐ **TIP!** Paint the monster in dragon colors. Or leave out the fire and paint him green. Then you'll have a cardboard crocodile!

97 MINI-MUMMIES

Mwahahaha! Scary toilet paper rolls!

SUPPLIES

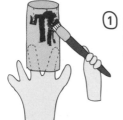

- 1 toilet paper roll
- black paint and paintbrush
- googly eyes
- glue
- gauze, cut into strips

① Paint the toilet paper roll black and allow it to dry fully.

② Stick on the eyes just above the midpoint of the roll.

③ Coat the entire roll with glue, leaving out the area around the googly eyes.

④ Wind the strips of gauze around the roll and press them down lightly so they stick. It's best to press down any loose bits of gauze with the paintbrush. Leave the area around the eyes free of gauze.

TIP! These also make great napkin rings for a Halloween party!

98 GLOW-IN-THE-DARK GHOSTS

Trying to be creepy? Impossible without glow-in-the-dark ghosts.

SUPPLIES

- paper
- glow-in-the-dark paint
- paintbrush
- black marker
- scissors

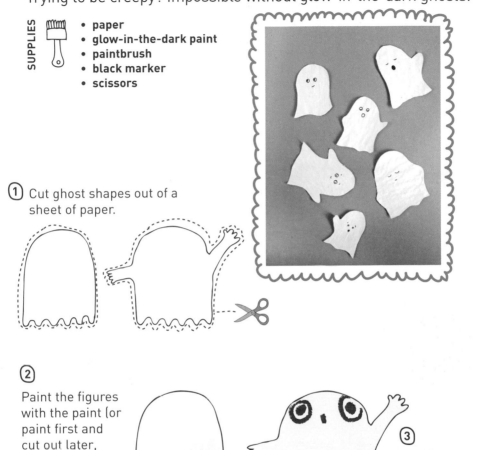

① Cut ghost shapes out of a sheet of paper.

② Paint the figures with the paint (or paint first and cut out later, whatever you'd like).

③ Once the paint has dried fully, draw a pair of eyes and a ghostly mouth.

④ Hang the ghosts up, turn off the light, and...boo!

⭐ **TIP!** Need signs or name tags for your Halloween party? Why not use these ghosts?

99 RATTLING SKELETON

Spooky!

SUPPLIES

- black and white drawing paper
- black marker
- cotton swabs
- glue
- scissors

① Cut a skull out of white paper and draw eyes, a nose, and a mouth on it.

② Glue the head and the cotton swabs on a sheet of black paper in the form of a funny skeleton.

100 DERANGED DRAGON

Ladies and gentleman, apples and pears, may I present to you the closing project of this book: a fantastic deranged dragon to say a fiery goodbye. See you later, alligator!

SUPPLIES

- **paper cups in a single color**
- **googly eyes**
- **split pins**
- **tissue paper in orange, red, white**
- **crafting foam rubber**
- **scissors**
- **glue**
- **permanent black marker**
- **hole punch and wooden skewer, optional**
- **extra decorations, optional: pipe cleaners, strips of tissue paper, stickers, etc.**

① Draw the mouth and nose of the dragon on either side of one cup and stick on the googly eyes.

② Using a hole punch, make two holes in the top of the cup, one on either side.

③ Slide a second cup part way into the first and affix it with two split pins, pushed through the holes punched in the last step. Keep going until you think the dragon is long enough.

⑤ ut the tissue aper in the hape of flames. wist them ogether and lue them in the ragon's mouth.

④ Cut triangles out of foam rubber and glue them onto the dragon's back.

⑥ Cut four feet out of foam rubber and glue them to the underside of the dragon on either side, front and back.

⑦ Cut out a tail and glue it to the last cup.

ALSO AVAILABLE

3D Art Lab for Kids
978-1-59253-815-7

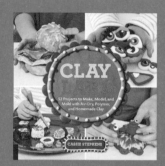

Clay Lab for Kids
978-1-63159-270-6

Paint Lab for Kids
978-1-63159-078-8

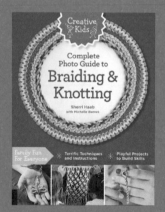

Creative Kids Complete Photo Guide to Braiding and Knotting
978-1-58923-937-1

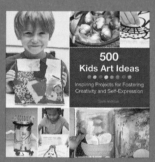

500 Kids Art Ideas
978-1-59253-985-7

Sharpie Art Workshop for Kids
978-1-63159-251-5